Touch and Expression

in Piano Playing

Clarence G. Hamilton

D1462565

Dover Publications, Inc.
Mineola, New York

Bibliographical Note

This Dover edition, first published in 2012, is an unabridged republication of
the work originally published by Oliver Ditson Company, Boston, in 1927.

Library of Congress Cataloging-in-Publication Data

Hamilton, Clarence G. (Clarence Grant), 1865–1935.
　　Touch and expression in piano playing / Clarence G. Hamilton.
　　　　p. cm.
　　Reprint; originally published: Boston : Oliver Ditson, 1927.
　　ISBN-13: 978-0-486-48828-8
　　ISBN-10: 0-486-48828-4
　　1. Piano—Instruction and study. I. Title.

　MT225.H23 2012
　786.2'193—dc23

2012018251

Manufactured in the United States by Courier Corporation
48828402
www.doverpublications.com

CONTENTS

PART I—TOUCH

PART II—EXPRESSION

FOREWORD

If he is to build a house, a carpenter must be supplied with adequate and properly sharpened tools; he must be expert in applying these tools to any demand that may arise; and he must have acquired the ability to follow out the plans of the architect, and to realize the latter's vision in the completed edifice. Just so, the pianist must possess fingers and muscles that are fitted to perform their intricate tasks; he must know how to manipulate the keys so as to produce every possible kind and gradation of tone; and he must be able to follow out the design of a given piece so as to realize in detail and as a whole the structure which was idealized in the composer's mind.

In the following pages I propose to treat of the means by which this final result is to be obtained. Given a person of normal conditions as to fingers, hand and arm, we shall proceed to inquire (1) in what ways these factors may be most effectively utilized to bring the fingers into contact with the keys, and (2) how such contact may be directed to the artistic interpretation of a composition. Of these two processes, the first has to do with *kinds of touch,* and the second with *the application of touch to expression.*

Touch

and

Expression

in Piano Playing

PART I. TOUCH

BEFORE considering the matter of touch, let us thoroughly free our minds from bias in favor of any one of the so-called "methods" of piano technic, however excellent such method may be. Let us remember that piano playing has been through a process of evolution during more than two hundred years, while players and teachers have stumbled along, experimenting in this way and that, many times propagating ideas that have afterward been supplanted by much better ones. Pupils of famous teachers, too, have often slavishly followed out their dicta, long after more enlightened methods have been invented by progressive players. Such masters as Liszt and Chopin, for instance, employed a new freedom of technic which amazed the adherents of the cut-and-dried systems of Hummel, Czerny and their followers, and which was correspondingly slow of general adoption.

In recent years, however, the searchlight of modern science has been directed upon piano playing, as upon most other subjects; with the result that, setting aside the empirical precepts that were formerly accepted as law and gospel, players and teachers have scientifically investigated the relative values for playing purposes of the muscles of the arm and hand, and have determined how these muscles may best be directed and coördinated to produce desired effects. Having such knowledge at his command, the individual player can judge for himself what kinds of touch to apply to a given passage, and can test intelligently the statements and suggestions of instructors and their "methods."

Useless Motions

Let us, at the outset, distinguish carefully between essential and non-essential muscular movements. To the latter class belong those gyrations, such as throwing the arms up in the air, or jerking the hand violently back from the wrist, which are employed either to "catch the crowd" or through ignorance of the keyboard mechanism, and which are as musically useless as were the antics of the old-time drum-major. With such movements may be listed the unnecessary pressure on a key after it has been sounded, which has no other result than to stiffen the performer's wrist, since it takes place after the hammer has fallen back from the string.

Relaxation

Before he proceeds to the study of piano touch, the student should acquire the ability to relax thoroughly all the muscles which have to do with playing; for without such ability he is as badly off as the sculptor who tries to fashion an image out of unyielding clay.

Next, he should gain such control over the playing factors that any given muscle or combination of muscles will respond instantly to his call, without interference from others.

APPLICATION.—To secure complete relaxation, sit before the keyboard and let the right arm hang down from the shoulder. Press the fingers downward, so that their tips approach the floor as nearly as possible, and then "let go."

A powerful muscle which is almost constantly in use is the *biceps* in the upper arm. Employing this muscle, raise the forearm, with the hand still relaxed, until the hand hangs over the keys with the fingers pointing downward as in illustration A, and nearly

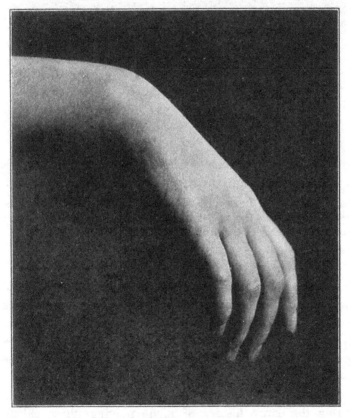

ILLUSTRATION A

touching them. Now allow the forearm to descend gently, so that the fingers rest lightly on the keys and the wrist is below them (illustration B).

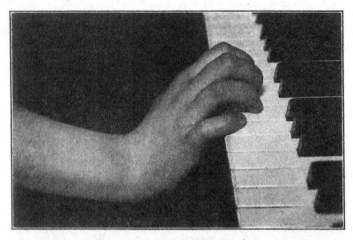

ILLUSTRATION B

Return to the former position above the keys, and lastly to the first position, with the arm at the side. These motions should be repeated a number of times with each hand.

Classes of Touch

Having thus established the basic condition of hand and arm, we are prepared to study tone-production. Since the direct medium for this lies in the depression of the keys by the fingers, we have then to discover just how this depression is best effected; or, in other words, what are the most useful and legitimate kinds of *touch*.

While many varieties of touch have been employed during the entire history of piano playing, those chiefly used by the modern pianist are four in number, distinguished by the different ways in which the energy that is transmuted through the finger-tips is generated in the muscular activities of hand, arm and shoulder.

Forearm Rotation

A valuable aid to all four of these touches is known

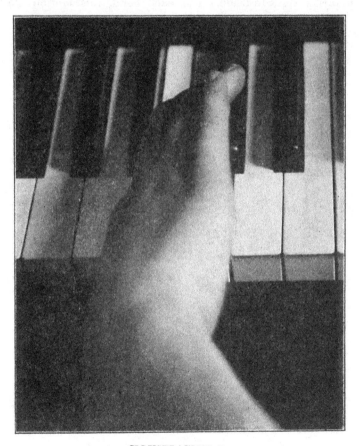

ILLUSTRATION C

as *forearm rotation*. We have all heard the expression "as easy as turning the hand over." But it has been discovered that this extremely simple movement, which necessarily involves also the forearm, may, if properly applied, generate a considerable degree of force to add to the pianist's stock-in-trade. For each hand, this motion may

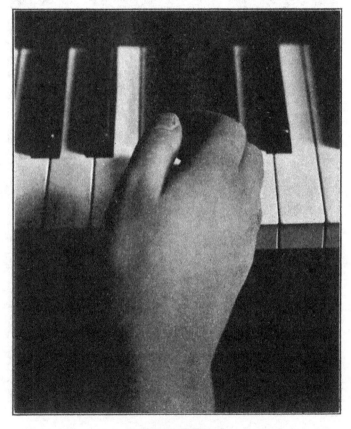

ILLUSTRATION D

be toward either the right or the left; and according to the rapidity of the movement is force added to the depression of the key.

APPLICATION.—Hold the right hand above the keyboard, as in illustration A, page 3. Now, lower the arm until the finger-tips rest on the treble keys *c, d, e, f, g*:  with the wrist held rather high, and the elbow hanging loosely at the side.

(1) Roll the forearm to the left, so that the thumb strikes and holds C. The hand should now be nearly perpendicular from the thumb up, with the fifth finger above the thumb, in the air. The striking motion should begin slowly and gradually accelerate until the key is sharply sounded—like the motion in cracking a whip (illustration C).

(2) With a similar motion, roll the forearm to the right so that the fifth finger strikes G, with the thumb nearly perpendicularly above it, (illustration D).

(3) Continue by rolling the forearm alternately to left and right, as before, using different degrees of force, from *p* to *f*, thus:

(4) Begin again on *c*, this time playing successively *c, d, e, f, g, f, e, d, c*. At each stroke rotate *slightly* to the right until *g* is sounded, when rotation to the left begins, and continues till *c* is again reached.

All of the above exercises should be repeated with the left hand.

Forearm rotation, then, means *to concentrate the force of each stroke directly over the key which is sounded*, so that the key thus becomes the centre of gravity of the hand·weight. The result illustrates the principle of mechanics that a direct force is more effective than an indirect one—a principle readily proved by trying to drive in a nail first by striking it with a sidewise blow, and then directly on the head.

I. THE FINGER TOUCH

In this, which requires the least amount of muscular activity of any of the touches, the key is depressed by pulling the finger down through the medium of a tendon attached to a muscle in the forearm.   When this tendon is again relaxed, the finger and key rise to their former position.

APPLICATION.—Let the right hand assume a normal playing position, in which the upper line of hand and wrist is about level,

ILLUSTRATION E

and the fingers rest on top of the keys *c—g*, (illustration E).   Make sure that the wrist is loose by raising and lowering it several times,

while the fingers retain their contact with the keys. Hold the fingers
firm,[1] and somewhat curved.

In the following exercises the use of staccato and legato are
respectively illustrated:

(1) *Staccato*:

Play each note by pressing the finger down quickly and relaxing
it the instant that the tone is heard, so that the finger *rides up on the
key*. The wrist should be kept perfectly quiet, and there should be
in it no consciousness of stiffness.

(2) *Legato*:

Sound each key as before, retaining just enough pressure, however, to prevent it from rising. Proceed to the next key by a slight
forearm rotation to the right, so that one key is released just as the
next is sounded.

History of This Touch

In the early pianos and their predecessors the clavi-
chords and harpsichords, the action was so light that the
finger touch was adequate for all demands. Teachers consequently emphasized the rule that the back of the hand
should be kept continually level, and as motionless as possible. Afterward, when the structure of the instrument demanded a heavier touch, the same rule was observed, but

---

[1]The word *firm* will be used throughout the book to indicate a condition of the muscles which, while somewhat elastic, is not rigid,
as in the case of a reed which may be slightly bent, but which, when
released, immediately returns to its former position.

additional force was gained by raising the fingers high and hitting the keys more vigorously. With the advent of pianists and teachers who had the courage to break this tradition—such as Chopin and Liszt—the weight and muscular force of hand and arm were utilized, and the "finger touch" was relegated mostly to the production of the lighter grades of tone.

At present, therefore, the finger touch is employed chiefly for performing delicate passage work or tenuous effects of accompaniment. So soon as louder tones are demanded, it merges into the more robust species of touch.

II. THE HAND TOUCH

Most frequently used of all the touches is the *hand touch*, so-called because its essential feature is the downward movement of the hand.

Hold your hand and forearm horizontally before you. Now throw the hand quickly downward as far as it will go. If unimpeded, it will exhaust its momentum in the free air.

But again, hold the hand just over a table, so that in their downward motion the fingers are stopped by the wooden surface. The momentum, thus suddenly interrupted, reacts upon the wrist, which, if allowed to do so, will jump upward. It is this upward tendency of the wrist which is an invariable mark of the hand touch.

APPLICATION.—Assume with the right hand the playing position on the keys *c-g* described on page 8, keeping the wrist loose and the fingers firm. Now, raising the thumb a quarter-inch or so from the key, throw the hand *over* and *into* the key *c*, so that when the thumb strikes the key, the wrist is jerked upward about an inch (see illustration F). Relax instantly, returning to the normal playing position. The result is a staccato. Exercise 3, page 9, may be practiced in this way by each hand, emphasizing the upward wrist movement at each stroke.

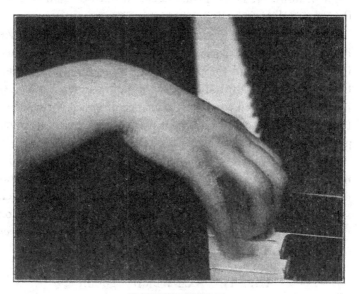

ILLUSTRATION F

For legato, practice Exercise 4, page 9, in a similar manner, but rotating slightly in the direction of each key as it is sounded. After each upward jerk, the wrist falls to its original level position.

Both the above exercises should be repeated many times, using different degrees of force, from *pp* to *ff*.

Four conditions should be carefully observed: (1) the upper arm should be kept continually loose, with the elbow at the side; (2) the forearm should be held up, so as to permit the free motion of the wrist; (3) the wrist should be kept perfectly relaxed; and (4) the fingers when playing should be held firm,—otherwise they will simply flop about on the keys. This condition of a relaxed wrist and firm fingers is the most difficult factor of the touch to obtain. Its neglect, however, is the prime cause of stiffness and lack of fluency in playing.

The hand touch has a wide range of usefulness, since it is employed in all sorts of rapid work—scales, arpeggios, intricate figures and the like—where more tone is required than can readily be produced by the finger touch alone. It is also well adapted to the performance of chords or octaves, from the light, accompaniment variety to those of more ponderous tone, such as the first chord in Beethoven's Op. 13.

Octaves are played slowly with the hand touch in the manner described above. In playing rapid octaves, however, the hand should be *tossed up* from the wrist at each stroke—not raised by the wrist muscles. For an illustration of rapid octaves, see Kullak's octave study, *From Flower to Flower*.

III. The Arm-Weight Touch

This touch is produced by suddenly dropping the forearm or full-arm (according to the degree of force required) so that the desired key or keys are pulled down in the descent. In its extreme form, the resultant position will be that shown in illustration B (page 4) with the hand and arm hanging from the key. As before, the movement starts from the normal playing position (see page 8); but the slight upward tendency of the wrist which occurs when the key is sounded is much more than counterbalanced by the arm-weight, so that the wrist falls instead of rising.

It is possible to play staccato with this touch by relaxing the finger as the tone is produced; but, owing to its essentially clinging character, the touch is better adapted to sustained or legato effects.

APPLICATION.—To play each note of the following exercise, hold the wrist at first high, so that the finger-tips barely touch the top of the keys. Suddenly relax the arm, sounding the given key as the arm descends; and finally hang on the key with the wrist below the keys. Return to the high wrist position, in order to play the next note. Observe that the wrist is kept relaxed throughout the exercise:

Repeat with the left hand, playing an octave lower.

The Combination of Hand and Arm-Weight Touches

For phrasing effects, the alternation of these two touches is invaluable. Consider, for instance, the case of two slurred notes. The first of these is given a solid basis by the arm-weight touch, after which the second is played by the hand touch with any desired degree of lightness or staccato.

APPLICATION.—Practice the following exercises by playing the first note of each pair with the arm-weight touch (D=down wrist) and the second with the hand touch (U=up wrist):

Independent slurring may be practiced by employing the two touches independently, in this exercise:

To play light, slurred runs, use the arm-weight on the first note, and let the wrist gradually rise (hand touch), until it floats into the air with the last note, thus:

Practice with the left hand an octave lower than as written.

How the two touches are aided by forearm rotation is shown in the following analysis of scale-technic. The letters R and L indicate rotation to right and left, respectively, while the letters D and U, written below, indicate arm-weight and hand touch, respectively. Dashes continue the preceding letter.

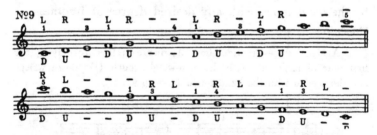

While the above is written out for the right hand, the movements of the left hand follow the same principle. It should be observed that after a downward movement the wrist rises gradually until the next down stroke, after which it again begins to rise.

These movements should now be applied to various scales, practicing with each hand by itself. Observe that the thumb is always used with the arm-weight touch, and that the hand touch is used with all the other notes, except where the finger starts the scale from its highest or lowest note.

Alternation of the two touches is well employed in playing legato octaves, where the hand touch is always used with the black keys and the arm-weight touch with a white key, when the latter directly follows a black key. Chromatic octaves especially illustrate this principle:

IV. The Full-Arm Touch

Upper arm, forearm, wrist, hand and fingers are linked firmly together for this touch, while the force is applied to the keys primarily by the shoulder muscle. Note, however, that this combination exists only during the act of key-depression, and that relaxation — especially of the wrist muscles — occurs *immediately afterwards*.

Application.—(1) Place the right hand in playing position, holding wrist and fingers firm. Now shrug up the shoulder as high as it will go. The entire arm and hand should rise with it, so that the fingers are two or three inches above the keys.

Suddenly force the shoulder downward, so that the thumb drives down *c* with a sharp blow. Instant relaxation produces a loud staccato, after which the hand returns to its quiet playing position. Repeat these motions, driving each finger down in turn.

Having thus studied the mechanism of the touch in an exaggerated form, proceed to its more normal use:

(2) With hand in playing position, hold the muscles firm, as before, and, without leaving the key, press down *c* with the thumb

repeatedly, playing staccato, and employing different degrees of force, from *p* to *f*. The amount of arm motion should be minimized. Take care that the consciousness of muscular activity resides primarily in the shoulder, and that the muscles are relaxed as the sound is heard. Repeat with each of the other fingers.

(3)   To play legato, the same action is used in depressing the key; but in the subsequent relaxation, just enough weight remains on the key to keep it firmly down. Beginning thus by sounding *c* with the thumb, proceed in order to *d, e, f,* and *g*, rotating slightly towards each key in turn, and, with each key-depression, feeling the firm combination of arm, wrist and hand, and also the action of the shoulder muscle.

As suggested in Application (1), this touch may be employed for playing chords or octaves where great dynamic power is required, as in an *sff*.   But its main usefulness lies rather in the direction of Applications (2) and (3), since, while controlling the finger by the powerful shoulder muscle, the player easily commands every possible gradation of force in the impact of the hammer on the string. Hence in melody playing, where such gradations are of especial importance, the full-arm touch is invaluable.

Here also attention may be drawn to the effect of finger position.   With any touch, when the fingers are considerably curved, the stroke is very direct and easily made detached, so that the tones become clear and precise.   Curved fingers, for instance, are advisable in playing the classics— Haydn, Mozart, etc.   With the flatter finger, however, the stroke is slower, and its clinging propensity tends toward the production of extreme legato: hence extended fingers are better adapted for the "singing" melody touch, which is further best controlled by the full-arm touch.   Chopin's sensuous melodies, consequently, are best rendered with this combination of extended fingers and full-arm touch.

V. SUMMARY

Summarizing the four touches as to their mechanism and fields of usefulness, we have the following:

1. *Finger Touch.* Loose wrist, finger action only. Reserved for the lightest grade of tone.

2. *Hand Touch.* Hand and fingers thrown into the keys from the wrist, which tends to rise at the stroke.

3. *Arm-Weight Touch.* Forearm and wrist fall, *pulling,* rather than *driving* the keys down.

Numbers 2 and 3 are primarily used for passage work.

4. *Full-Arm Touch.* Arm and hand linked together at moment of key-depression. Employed for heavy work and for singing melodies.

All these touches are frequently aided by forearm rotation.

Minimizing Movements

From the above description of the muscular activities involved in the various touches, the reader may have gathered the impression that modern piano playing consists in a series of extravagant gyrations of hand and arm. Observe, however, that what has been described should, in its finished state, take place largely in the player's mind, and that its outward manifestation should be comparatively slight. For just as an infant, when learning to walk, balances himself painfully first on one foot and then on the other, so the player must analyze each motion consciously, and with exaggerated gesture, before he can proceed with ease.   Having selected the right touch and acquired the right habits, however, he may minimize the muscular motions, so that each muscle performs its task almost imperceptibly,—just as the older child has learned to walk or run with but the slightest suggestion of the complicated muscular movements which he has learned to perform.   So the expert player retains, as a rule, a quiet, level position of the hand, allowing the wrist to rise or fall only slightly as the touch demands, and rotating just as slightly from one side to the other.

Moreover, having acquired a command over the different species of touch, the player arrives at the point where he instinctively chooses just the right species for the passage in hand—the finger touch for very light runs, the arm-weight touch for melodies, etc.   Thus all the touches should coöperate as though they were parts of a well-adjusted and well-oiled machine.

Other Touches

Special kinds of touches are often mentioned which are really but phases of the fundamental touches described above.   Such are the so-called *legato* and *staccato* touches, also the *pressure* or *melody* touches, both of which are practically identical with our full-arm touch.

Raising the Fingers

Again, the question may arise as to whether the fingers should be raised in playing, and if so, to what extent.   To this we may reply that the modern pianist seldom, if ever, raises the fingers merely to secure greater force—since it has been discovered that such force may be better obtained through other means. On the other hand, there is no reason why the fingers should be eternally "glued" to the keys. Sometimes, indeed, greater clearness and precision may be gained by slightly raising the fingers.[1] If so, why not raise them! I have had pupils whose tendency to overlap the notes could be remedied in no other way. Let us rather take as our maxim that, in the interest of ease in performance, all unnecessary and futile elevation of the fingers—or, for that matter, of the hand or arm—should be avoided.

VI. PEDALS

Our treatment of touch would be far from complete without a mention of pedal technic. Here again the same principle of relaxation should be applied. Keep the feet in readiness on or near the pedals, and when the latter are brought into use, eliminate all useless or awkward motions. When the right foot is on the damper pedal, be sure that no pressure whatever is exerted, since such pressure may be just enough to raise the dampers slightly from the strings, and so produce a blur of tone.[2]

In applying the pedal, depress it always *to its full extent,* by a quick downward movement made from the ankle joint; and finally release it by *relaxing* the pressure as suddenly as it was applied, not by pulling up the foot.

[1]This is especially the case with consecutive double notes.

[2]I have heard otherwise good pianists unconsciously (?) spoil their music in this way, especially if the pedal has an unusually light spring.

It is a safe rule to depress the pedal just *after* sounding the note or chord that is to be sustained, except when the latter is very short or stands alone. Observance of this rule will prevent a disagreeable overlapping of the melody tones.

APPLICATION.—For pedal technic, I know of no better exercise than the following, suggested to me by that sterling teacher, Mr. Arthur Foote, an exercise of glorious simplicity:

All the notes are played by the one finger. Sound each note sharply, and count two to it. The pedal is depressed on each second beat, and rises exactly as the next note is sounded. The finger may release its key as soon as the pedal is firmly down. As a result, a perfect legato between the tones is secured.

PART II. EXPRESSION

I. Values

WHILE the orchestral instruments, such as the violins, horns, oboes, etc., are ordinarily required to play only one voice-part at a time, the piano, in common with the organ, must, as a rule, play several voice-parts at once, and must even at times simulate a full orchestra. If piano music be properly interpreted, therefore, each of these parts must be given its proper place in the entire scheme. Just as a painter, when depicting a rolling landscape, distinguishes between its different distances—the light blue of the sky, the purple of the far-off hills, the more distinct hues of the middle distance, finally the bright greens of the fore-ground —so the pianist must give to each of the component parts of a composition its due value, vividly bringing out the central features, and subordinating those which are merely incidental.

For this purpose, he should make a discriminating use of the various touches, each of which may correspond in his mind with some orchestral instrument. The finger touch, for example, may be likened to the delicate flute, the hand touch to the agile violin, the arm-weight touch to the bright clarinet, and the full-arm touch to the sonorous horn.

Values in Contrapuntal Music

Just how these touches are to be combined and con-

trasted will depend on the type of the given composition.
A more homogeneous treatment, for instance, will be ac-
corded a polyphonic piece, such as one of Bach's fugues,
since here the voice-parts are theoretically of equal value.
But in an artistic interpretation this equality is continually
upset by the fact that, while all the parts should be played
with melodic expression, whatever is of special thematic
value should come to the fore—in a fugue, the principal
subject or answer, next, the counter-subject, next, any inter-
esting recurrent figure.   Consider, as an illustration, the
following passage from Bach's three-part fugue, Vol. I,
No. 21 of the *Well-Tempered Clavichord*.   Here the principal subject in the lower voice (1) is of primary importance, while the counter-subject in the middle voice (2) and
the little figure which darts in on top (3) vie with one
another for second place:

(No. 12)
Fugue from W.T.C. Vol. 1, No. 21   J. S. BACH

Consequently, while the subject proper is played with

the full-arm touch, this touch is more or less modified by using the hand or arm-weight touch in the subordinate melodies.

Values in Harmonic Music

Coming now to the harmonic type of music, we find this in its simplest form when a melody or running passage is supported by chords, either broken or massed together. But even in this case three different values may be distinguished, namely, the melody proper, the progression of the bass notes, and the intervening chord combinations. Often to these three a fourth part is added, closely connected to the melodic part, as in this passage from Chopin's *Valse brillante,* Op. 34, No. 2:

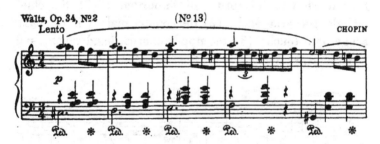

Here the upper sustained A's should be played with the full-arm touch, the bass notes by the arm-weight touch, while the running melodic part and the accompanying chords are played by the hand touch.

Such a union of four voices occurs in all sorts of melodic and harmonic combinations. Consider, for instance, Schumann's *Romance,* Op. 28, No. 2, where the melodic duet is played with full-arm touch by both thumbs, while on both sides of it the accompaniment is delicately shadowed by the finger or hand touch:

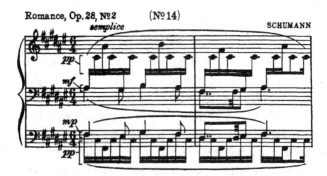

In the following passage from Liszt's third *Liebestraum,* the four values are more clearly defined, calling upon all four touches in this order of importance: (1) the chief melody, full-arm touch; (2) the counter melody in the bass, arm-weight touch; (3) the upper chords, hand touch; and (4) the arpeggiated chords, finger touch:

Whatever the combination, therefore, the pianist should carefully consider the different values involved, should decide on their order of importance, and should choose for the expression of each the species of touch which seems best adapted to place it in its proper perspective.

In such an estimate, the student should remember that dynamic marks such as *p, mf, f* are merely general in their application, and that they do not refer to individual voice-parts. The last example, quoted from Liszt, for instance, may be marked *piano*, a composite effect produced by playing the melody and bass *mf*, while the accompaniment is played *pp*.

Observe also that the loudness or softness indicated by these marks should continue until they are contradicted. A subordinate *crescendo* and *diminuendo* may occur in a passage that, as a whole, is *piano* in effect; but with the introduction of a *forte*, a new tonal range is indicated.

II. PULSATION IN MUSIC

Having thus adjusted his values, the pianist should now call upon every factor that will invest his interpretation with vitality and interest; for he cannot successfully conduct his auditors through an arid plain, where only the stubble of technic meets their view. Rather, it is his pleasant task to lead them along a road bordered with colorful flowers, constantly ascending to greater heights, until on the mountain top the full glory of the view for which they have been striving breaks upon them. In other words, music, like speech, is a progressive art, proceeding from one climax to another, each clothed in details of ever increasing interest.

Normal and Abnormal Conditions

During this progress, the player has to deal with certain normal conditions, which may easily be stated. But his mettle is best asserted in his treatment of the multiple unusual ways with which a composer varies the monotony, and adds attractive novelties. In our study of the factors of expression, therefore, let us first observe the conditions and principles of regularity in composition, and then glance at those irregularities which are so numerous and varied as to defy complete analysis.

Beats

First of all, then, is the ever recurring pulsation or *beat*, which is the vital factor in music. For just as life conditions are determined by the strength, evenness and frequency of the heart-throb, so is the character of the music determined by the emphasis, regularity and rapidity with which the pulsations are presented by the player.

Let us observe, however, that in music beats are never treated as individual entities, but that they occur invariably in groups, with one beat predominant over the others. Of these groups the smallest is the *measure*, with a fundamental structure that is either *duple* or *triple*.

Here let us sharply distinguish between the so-called *bar-measure*, which lasts from one bar to the next, and the true *phrase-measure*, which regularly proceeds from a point in one bar-measure to a corresponding point in the next. For, in musical notation, a bar is in reality an *accent*, indicating that the following beat has a strong pulsation. Now, inasmuch as it is more natural to work up to such a pulsation than to begin with it, the bar line is most apt to occur in the middle or just before the end of a phrase-measure than at its beginning. Thus in duple meter the phrase-measure often consists of the beats: 2|1 than of | 1 2 | ;

while in triple meter the phrase-measure is more often
2 3 | 1, or 3 | 1 2 than | 1 2 3.   But note again that a phrase-
measure regularly ends in one bar-measure at the exact point
where it began in the preceding bar-measure.

As an illustration of the statements just made, let us
now examine Chopin's little *Prelude*, Op. 28, No. 7:

Prelude, Op. 28, №7   (№ 16)   CHOPIN
Period

Here each phrase-measure evidently involves a rise and
fall in the strength of pulsation, so that the beats follow one
another in the order—*weak* STRONG *weak, weak* STRONG
weak, etc: ‿ ‗ ‿ , ‿ ‗ ‿ .

While recognizing that, as a rule, the chief accent of the measure
falls on the first beat, the student should be on the alert to detect
the error of misplaced bars, which has sometimes been made even
by the leading composers. A notable instance of this error occurs
in Chopin's *Nocturne*, Op. 9, No. 2, where, as he has written it, the
chief accent is made to fall wrongly in the middle of each bar-

measure. In the following excerpt, the dotted lines represent the correct barring, while the unbroken bars are those given by Chopin:

Another instance is found in Schumann's *Novelette*, Op. 21, where the bars should come before the third beats as the composer wrote it. Even the impeccable Mendelssohn sometimes nods in this respect, as is shown in his *Song without Words*, Op. 38, No. 16, where the bars should be placed in the middle of each measure as Mendelssohn has it.

Accents

Let us now pause to consider what kinds of accents are at the pianist's disposal. As a whole, these may be divided into two classes, of which the first is the *dynamic* or *force* accent. This, which consists simply in playing the stressed note louder than its fellows, is employed whenever vitality is the prime requisite. Chopin's *Military Polonaise*, Op. 40, No. 1, for instance, demands a strong dynamic accent on each first beat:

In contrast to this species is the *agogic* or *time* accent, where a note is given prominence by slightly prolonging its time-value. Indicated in this way, the phrase-measure consists of slightly irregular beats, of which the chief (the first of the bar-measure) is the longest. Thus in $\frac{3}{4}$ meter, the beats may be 3̆ | 1̄ 2̆, 3̆ | 1̄ 2̆, etc. (⌣ = short beat, − = long beat.) Poetic and tenderly emotional compositions, such as Chopin's nocturnes, call for this form of accent. The *Prelude*, Op. 28, No. 7 (page 27) may be treated as an example of its use.

Observe also that the amount of prolongation of the beat will correspond to the fluctuation of the sentiment. In the above *Prelude*, for instance, the first beat of most of the measures is only infinitesimally prolonged; but at the chief climax, in measure 12, the first chord is considerably more stressed, and is further emphasized by arpeggiating it.

In actual practice, however, the two kinds of accent are constantly used in combination, either one becoming dominant according to the demands of the piece. Referring again to the Chopin *Prelude*, for instance, there is a touch of the dynamic accent at the beginning of each even-numbered measure: 2, 4, 6, etc. Chopin's *Nocturne in F major*, Op. 15, No. 1, presents a striking example of the interplay of the two forms of accent, since the poetic Part I (measures 1-24) and its counterpart (measures 49-74) call primarily for the agogic accent, while the stormy Part II (measures 25-48) requires the dynamic accent.

III. PHRASES AND THEIR COMBINATION

Ordinarily a phrase-measure deals with but a single musical *figure*, which, when continued in the following measure, becomes a complete *motive*. In the Chopin *Pre-lude*, Op. 28, No. 7, for instance, the two-measure motive consists of the two figures:

Again, the question-like effect of this motive is answered in the next two measures, the whole constituting a four-measure *phrase*. Similarly, a phrase answered by another may produce a *period*, and two such periods may produce a *section*. The above Chopin *Prelude* well illustrates this structure, since it consists of a single section, which is made up of two eight-measure periods, each of which in turn consists of two four-measure phrases.

Now it is for the pianist to determine just what is the relation of each phrase to its following phrase, and ultimately to the whole piece; consequently, what degree of intensity it should receive. Each phrase and period should have its own climax; and these individual points of stress should work up to the climax of the section. Finally, these "sectional" climaxes contribute their quota toward the climax of the entire composition, which naturally occurs at or toward the end. In a bravura piece, for instance, such as Mendelssohn's *Rondo Capriccioso* or Chopin's *Ballade in G minor*, the whole composition ends in a blaze of glory; while in a dreamy piece, such as Chopin's *Nocturne*, Op. 15, No. 1, the period of "storm and stress" may be followed by a restful close.

In a complex composition, the monotony of exactly balancing phrases is usually arrested by the extension, or, less often, the abbreviation of certain phrases. Lingering pieces, such as Mendelssohn's *Songs Without Words*, gravitate towards the lengthening of phrases, as in No. 1, where the second phrase (after the introduction) is extended from four to nine measures.   The contraction of a phrase, on the other hand, has an abrupt effect, as at the beginning of the second movement of Schubert's *Sonata,* Op. 120:

Both of these phrases are irregular, since each is but three and a half measures long, instead of the expected four measures. But whereas the first phrase simply omits the three unessential introductory notes, the second is cut off a beat and a half too soon, as though Schubert were in a hurry to end it!

A word of warning should be given the student against the misleading phrase-marks found in many so-called "standard editions" of the classics. Through the carelessness of composer or publisher or both, slurs have often been introduced which are as absurd as though marks of punctuation—commas, periods, etc.—were posted at regular intervals in a piece of poetry, regardless of their effects. For instance, observe this melody from the last movement of Beethoven's Sonata, Op. 2, No. 1, in which the erroneous slurs (copied from a standard edition) are placed above the notes, while the correct phrasing is indicated beneath them:

Fortunately, publishers are giving more attention to this important matter, so that most of the classics are now available edited by experts.[1] The student should strive to employ only these more authoritative editions, and should even then test their value in the light of his own taste and sense of fitness.

IV. IRREGULAR ACCENTS

An important device for securing variety is the introduction of a special accent which conflicts with the normal accent of the measure. Some dance rhythms, indeed, are based on just such conflicts, especially the mazurka, where the chief accent often comes on the third beat, and occasionally on the second beat. For example, in Moszkowski's *Mazurka*, Op. 10, No. 3, note the third-beat accent in the first two measures of this passage:

In such a case, it is quite possible to stress both regular

[1]The volumes of the *Musicians Library* (Oliver Ditson Company) furnish an example of such careful and reliable editing.

and irregular accents by employing the different species: in the above passage, for instance, the agogic accent for the first beat, which continues the regular swing of the piece, precedes the sharply contrasting dynamic accent on the third beat.

Irregular Rhythms

Assuming that regular rhythm involves the presence on the principal beats of notes that are as long or longer than those on the subordinate beats, it is evident that such regularity is upset when the longer note occurs in a subordinate position. If for instance, instead of the regular rhythm of triple measure: we have the irregular rhythm we instinctively resent the intrusion of the long note on the weak beat. Consequently this note often justifies its presence by a special emphasis, as in Scharwenka's popular *Polish Dance*:

Polish Dance, Op. 3, №1   (№ 22)

X. SCHARWENKA

As befits the mazurka character of this piece, a conflicting accent occurs on the second beat of the first two measures, and (in lesser degree) on the third beat of the next two measures.

While such a long note frequently calls for a sharp accent in strongly rhythmic music, it should be more subtly

treated in music of a lyric nature, since, as with the agogic
accent, its very length gives it sufficient prominence. In
Schubert's *Impromptu*, Op. 142, No. 2, for instance, the
measure accent takes decided precedence over that suggested
by the longer note on the second beat:

Impromptu, Op. 142, №2   (№ 23)
Allegretto   SCHUBERT

pp sempre legato

We may state as a general principle, therefore, that the player
should give most prominence to the regular measure accent unless
a conflicting accent is especially indicated by the composer or is
clearly demanded by the spirit of the composition.

Syncopation

A long note occurring directly after the measure accent
may have the effect of a kind of reverberation or reinforce-
ment of that accent. Schubert is especially fond of this
device, often employing it in the accompaniment, while the
melodic part proceeds in regular rhythm—an effect which
runs through his entire *Theme and Variations*, Op. 142, No.
3, as in the second variation:

Impromptu, Op. 142, №3   (№ 24)
Andante   SCHUBERT

p

In this case, the regular accent and that of the following chord should be equally stressed, since the two accented notes together really complete a broken chord.

The device just described is a form of the important musical factor known as *syncopation,* which occurs whenever a note or chord sounded on a weak beat is prolonged into the following strong beat. Inasmuch as this syncopated note thus takes the place of the note which would regularly come on the strong beat, it should receive the latter's accent.

Syncopation is a favorite device for varying the monotony of regular rhythmic periods. Schumann, an adept in its use, often syncopates entire chords, as in his *Grillen,* from Op. 12:

The syncopated chords are marked by an asterisk (*).

Such syncopation may result in so radical a change of meter as to demand new barring, as at the eighth measure of the passage just quoted.

Unless, too, the syncopation is defined by occasional normal accents, it may defeat its own object by establishing a new regular rhythm of its own. Schumann fell into this trap in the first movement of his *Faschingsschwank aus Wien*, Op. 26, where this syncopation pervades an entire section:

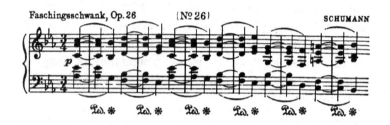

In listening to this passage, since there is nothing to prevent, the auditor assumes that each syncopated note comes on the regular measure accent, so that he hears the regular rhythm: ♩ ♩ ♩ ♩ , instead of what Schumann intended. Under the circumstances, the best that the pianist can do is to depress the pedal on the first beat of each measure, as indicated above, thus slightly reinforcing the tone (page 63).

More subtle forms of syncopation occur where a note is thus treated in one part while regular rhythms occur in the others. This is a favorite device for securing melodic contrast in polyphonic music, as in the following excerpt from the first fugue in Bach's *Well-Tempered Clavichord*. Observe how syncopated notes answer one another in the upper and middle voices:

Fugue from W.T.C.,Vol.I, № 1   (№ 27)   BACH

An instance of syncopation in the accompaniment has been shown in the reinforcing accent, that is illustrated on page 34. Conversely, melodic notes may be syncopated over an accompaniment in regular rhythm, as at the beginning of Chopin's *Nocturne in G minor*, where the initiatory D draws attention to the lyric melody which it starts:

Nocturne, Op. 37, № 1   (№ 28)   CHOPIN
Andante sostenuto

A beautiful example of such a syncopation in the bass occurs in the theme of the second movement of Beethoven's *Sonata Appassionata*:

Sonata, Op. 57   (№ 29)   BEETHOVEN
Andante

Syncopation, as has been said, is essentially anticipatory of important notes. This effect is reversed, however,

when a note is *delayed* in its utterance. In the following
passage at the beginning of Chopin's *Nocturne in C minor*,
the first two notes of the melody would regularly occur on
the first and third beats of measure 1, and the third and
fourth notes respectively on the first and second beats of
measure 2. Observe that the second melody note in measure 2 serves also as a syncopation:

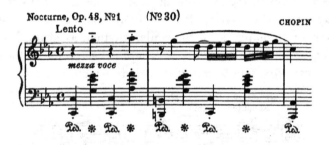

Like syncopated notes, delayed notes should be especially
stressed.

Special Accents

Occasionally a composer introduces a special accent to
vary the even rhythmic flow, or to surprise the listener. In
the works of Beethoven and his contemporaries (particularly
Clementi) we find frequent accents of this kind, indicated
by the term *sforzando* (*sf*), meaning *forced*. In his very
first published sonata, for instance, Beethoven precedes the
final cadence of the first movement by three explosions on
the weak beats:

Sonata, Op. 2, №1   (№ 31)   BEETHOVEN
Allegro

Besides these prescribed accents, however, the player should constantly be on the lookout for any peculiar note or chord which might pass unnoticed or even sound like a mistake on the player's part unless duly stressed. In this decorative run from Chopin's *Nocturne in E♭*, for instance, the unexpected C♭, if slightly accented, gives distinction to the whole passage:

Nocturne, Op. 9, №2   (№ 32)   CHOPIN

Similarly, in Debussy's *Clair de lune,* on the return of the first theme, a C♭ added to the supporting chord on the second beat results in a new harmonic flavor, and should therefore be given prominence:

Clair de Lune   (№ 33)   DEBUSSY
Andante

V. Dynamic Contrasts

During its evolution from the weak-toned clavichord and spinet, the piano has gradually grown in tonal capacity and sustaining power, until a vast difference now exists between the *ppp* and *fff* possible to the modern concert grand. Consequently, while only feeble dynamic contrasts were at the command of the early clavier composers, such contrasts have grown steadily in importance, especially from the time of Beethoven, until they have finally become one of the most potent factors of expression.

This growth in dynamic possibilities, too, has resulted in continual experimentation as to the means of handling the various grades of intensity; with the result that the different touches described in Part I have supplemented the original finger touch, which formerly sufficed. Indeed, it would require only a brief attack of the modern muscular technic to effect the complete ruin of the delicate and fragile pianos of the early nineteenth century.

Despite his uncouth manners and his defiance of conventions, Beethoven was eagerly welcomed in the most select circles of his day. And why? Because when his fingers touched the keyboard, his hearers were thrilled by an unheard-of wealth of expression, largely derived from tonal contrasts. Reacting upon his published compositions, these contrasts are indicated by the mark *sf*, sprinkled through the pages, by the words *crescendo, diminuendo, rinforzando* and the like, in short, by an unprecedented array of dynamic varieties.

Thus Beethoven set the pace for following composers, until in the theatric glitter of Liszt's accomplishments the range of intensity of the strengthened piano is tested to its capacity in either direction.

As he acquires a mastery over this tonal wealth, the piano student should at the same time cultivate a control over his resources that will insure a constant reserve power. Even the most brilliant piece, when its every note is rendered *fortissimo,* becomes merely a ceaseless din, exasperating to the hearer. Furthermore, to begin a piece at the limit of one's strength precludes any further increase, and thus nullifies those climaxes which are the focal points of interest.

Careful study of values (page 21) will help to secure the proper perspective. But even in brilliant compositions, the pianist should paint his high colors upon a low-toned background. For just as the height of the hills of Mt. Desert is enhanced by their sheer rise from the sea level, so the dynamic contrasts in music are rendered more vivid if they stand out from quiet surroundings.

Contrasts of Mood

Dependent on extreme dynamic effects are those compositions of the salon type in which whole sections are sharply contrasted in *piano* and *forte.* Perhaps the most famous forerunner of many such modern works is the *Invitation to the Dance* of C. M. von Weber—whose extensive operatic experience fitted him for the sensational qualities shown in this, as in others of his works, notably the *Concertstück,* Op. 79. In the *Invitation to the Dance* we find a seductively romantic introduction, followed by this brilliant waltz theme:

Invitation to the Dance, Op. 65 (№ 34) Von WEBER
Allegro vivace

A tenderly soft section (*molto dolce*) immediately ensues, beginning a series of constantly shifting emotional moods which work up to a final crash that is mitigated by a suave postlude.

Of the long line of similarly highly-spiced concert pieces which followed, we may instance Liszt's *Valse Impromptu in A♭*, Moszkowski's *Air de Ballet*, Op. 36, No. 5, and Rubinstein's *Valse Caprice in E♭*.

An effective class of pieces in which the contrasts are less numerous are those of the A B A structure, in which the B division has a markedly different dynamic range from the others. Sometimes, as in Chopin's *Fantasie Impromptu*, Op. 66, the B division is in lower tonal values than the A's; more often, however, the A divisions are in quiet, lyric style, while the B division works up to a frenetic climax. Such a one is Chopin's *Nocturne*, Op. 15, No. 1 (page 29). Another fine example is Sgambati's *Nocturne in B minor*, Op. 20, where the connection between the extreme moods is made with especial cleverness.

Particularly in the shorter forms, a single mood may prevail throughout the piece. Lively dances lend themselves readily to the expression of continuously joyous moods. As a noteworthy example, we may again cite Chopin's *Polonaise in A major*, Op. 40, No. 1, where the pomp of military panoply gleams throughout, reinforced during the middle section by a trumpet-like melody.

At the opposite pole stand those vague, impressionistic pictures of which Debussy was past master, in which the prevailing low tones are rarely much intensified, and in which the mystic atmosphere suggests an almost continual use of the soft pedal. Debussy's *Claire de lune* (page 39) typifies this style, as also does its twin from the North, Palmgren's *May Night*.

Between these extremes lie various shades of emotional moods, of which the most conspicuous are lyric pieces such as the delicate cameos of Grieg, the picturesque sketches of MacDowell, and especially Mendelssohn's perennial *Songs without Words*, in which quiet moods, such as those of No's. 1, 9 and 25, contrast with agitated outbursts, as in No's. 8 and 21. In his *Des Abends*, Op. 12, No. 1, Schumann has given us an ideal expression of lyric beauty, in which the evenness of the song-part is charmingly diversified by the cross rhythms of the accompaniment.

Dealing with such examples of a single mood, the student should consider its restricted tonal range, and thus guard against exaggeration, especially of the quiet, restful piece, by too strenuous crescendos or too explosive chords. Let him treat a *genre* piece by Debussy, for instance, as a bit of delicate china, which may be shattered by a violent blow.

Contrasts of Details

Distinguished from such general contrasts as have been presented are the instances where a note or short group of notes are in direct contrast to those adjoining.

Treated in this way, a single chord may acquire extraordinary significance. We are all familiar with the "surprise" chord in Haydn's *G major Symphony*, which, interrupting the music's placid flow, is calculated, as Haydn put it, to "make the ladies jump." Of different nature is the dominant chord in the second movement of Beethoven's *Sonata*, Op. 10, No. 1 (measure 45), which is strongly emphasized since it represents the entire development section of the sonata-allegro form:

In the same movement are examples of "echoing" effects, where an assertive group is answered from a distance:

Here is an example from Mozart of echoes in different registers:

Such short contrasting groups may, however, represent not so much an echo as two supplementary moods. Bee-

thoven suggested that his *Sonata,* Op. 90 was a contest between the head and the heart, an idea embodied in the
answering phrases of the opening measures.

For picturesque purposes, too, quick contrasts are invaluable. Can we imagine a more thrilling effect on the
piano than that at the close of MacDowell's *Eagle,* Op. 32,
No. 1, where, from his crag above the "wrinkled sea" the
bird dashes down *fff* upon his prey:

The Eagle, Op. 32, №1   (№ 38)   MACDOWELL

Value of Rests

In the foregoing passage we observe also the value of
the *rest* as a means of emphasizing dynamic contrasts.
Coming from an instant of complete silence, the final chords
are a veritable "bolt from the blue." It is related that
Mozart, when asked what is the finest effect in music, replied
"no music," meaning rests. Frequent rests in his music
show how he practically applied this theory, as in the passage from his *Fantasia in C minor,* quoted above. Rests,
then, may enhance dramatic moments, or they may furnish
breathing spaces in which the auditor's curiosity as to what
may follow is keenly alert.

A prevalent error into which piano students fall is that of hurrying over rests, or nullifying them by retaining the damper pedal through them. On the contrary, a rest should be given more, rather than less than its prescribed time, especially when it follows a slur. Unfortunately, rests are sometimes inserted in modern music to represent technical, instead of actual pauses, since the damper pedal is evidently to be kept down during their duration. The last four measures in Liszt's *Gondoliera*, is an instance in point, since the pedal is retained through the rests in the first two of these measures. The student will do well to avoid such a liberty except when it is clearly called for in the text.

Direct Repetition

Often a short passage is directly repeated, as though the composer wished thus to call attention to its beauty before proceeding on his way. In this case the repetition will be given some mark of distinction, perhaps by playing it more softly than its original, as in Ravel's *Sonatine*, second movement:

Sonatine — Mouvement de Menuet — (№ 39) — RAVEL

In a transitional passage leading to a new idea or the return of an old one, such repetitions may in some way be increasingly emphasized, as in measures 45-52 of the movement just quoted. Of course the mere repetition of a technical figure, such as is frequent in piano études, does not ordinarily call for especial attention.

VI. Dynamic Shadings

Strong dynamic contrasts, as we have seen, are employed chiefly for sensational and dramatic effects. Under ordinary circumstances, however, such effects should be avoided by the player in favor of more carefully graded *nuances*, and an artistic smoothness of interpretation which requires that strong pulsations be approached by a gradual increase of tone that is often complemented by a corresponding decrease. Even the measure accent should be considered to be the culminating point of a short but gradual growth in intensity, and not as an unpremeditated blow. Wrong and right uses of dynamics are indicated in this example from Beethoven's Op. 2, No. 1:

Sonata, Op. 2, Nº1   (Nº 40)   BEETHOVEN

Thus the underlying progress of music is marked by a succession of tonal waves of all degrees of intensity, the longer waves broken up into those of shorter lengths, and these latter traversed by ripples, each a measure in length. It is only when these waves meet with an opposing force that the dynamic contrasts which we have studied occur.

Since it is least in importance and frequently but marks the rhythmic swing, the measure wave is often so minimized as to be merged imperceptibly into the phrase wave. Again, a still broader effect is gained by treating the whole phrase as a crescendo, to be answered by a diminuendo in the following phrase. As given on page 27, for instance, the Chopin *Prelude* has but one wave for each eight-measure period, divided between its two component phrases.

Grades of Climaxes

Infinite degrees of shading, too, may be employed in the individual phrases. Tchaikovsky, in the first movement of his *Sixth Symphony*, indicates these subtle gradations of tone: *pppp* ⎯⎯ *pp* ⎯⎯ *pppp* . So one set of balancing phrases may be followed by another of greater or less intensity. In the Chopin *Prelude* just mentioned, for instance, the second set of eight measures is, as a whole, more intense than the first set, with the greatest stress of all in measure 12. Similarly in an extended composition the pianist will contrast or intensify whole sections or periods, thus constantly whetting the auditor's curiosity and interest to the very end.

Following the structure of the piece, too, the player will correspondingly vary the length of his crescendos and diminuendos. Often two short emotional waves precede one of longer compass: as in Chopin's *Military Polonaise*, Op. 40, No. 1, where there is a complete crescendo and diminuendo in each of the first two pairs of measures, followed by a longer, more intense crisis which occupies four measures.

Some climaxes, too, are produced by a very quick

tonal increase, so that a brilliancy is attained that reminds one of the crackling of fireworks: witness those in the Chopin *Polonaise* just cited. Others, on the contrary, move steadily onward with the cumulative power of the long ocean rollers: witness the inexorable onward sweep of Beethoven's *Funeral March* (from Op. 26). While quick climaxes furnish plenty of opportunity for the pianist to display his technical brilliancy, it is in the slowly moving crescendo or diminuendo that his reserve power is especially called upon: for then the crescendo should advance by almost imperceptible degrees until, when near the summit, the pent-up tonal avalanche is unloosed. In representing such a crescendo, curved lines should replace the ordinary straight ones, thus: *p* ⎯⎯⎯⎯⎯⎯ *ff*

Conversely, in a long diminuendo the original intensity should be decreased very gradually until the final drop, the whole represented by the curved lines: *f* ⎯⎯⎯⎯⎯⎯ *pp*
As an example of this latter effect, we may cite the final eight measures of Grieg's *Berceuse*, Op. 38, No. 1.

Correlation of Phrases

While, as has been said, the pianist should recognize the length of the phrases, he should also make clearly evident the connection or lack of connection between them. In music of a dance-like character, phrases are generally quite distinct, sometimes even separated by rests. Also in formal music, such as that of the classic sonata writers, endings of sections, at least, are unmistakably obvious.

With the advent of nineteenth century romanticism, however, there is a growing tendency to substitute vague outlines for the clarity of classicism; consequently phrases are more closely connected, so that one often runs into another without perceptible break, the two linked by a continuous melodic outline, by a sustained accompaniment, or by connecting figures. Consider, for instance, a modern work such as Debussy's *Clair de lune.* Here all the above factors are utilized to create that shimmering atmosphere which floats steadily on without break.

Let the player be prepared, therefore, to make his phrase-connections fit the piece in hand, and even on occasion to eliminate all phrase divisions, merely shadowing them in the rise and fall of the measures.

Effect of Varying Pitch

In ascending any scale, the number of vibrations of the individual tones rapidly increase in number. If a^1, for instance, has 435 vibrations per second, its octave a^2 has twice that number, or 870 vibrations. But as vibrations increase in number, the strength of tone tends to diminish. It is quite evident in the piano, for instance, that the long, thick bass strings tend to produce a louder tone than the very short, thin upper ones. Hence, to preserve the proper balance in tonal strength, we normally observe the principle that *a rise in pitch demands a crescendo, and a fall in pitch a diminuendo.*

Applying this principle to a melody of varying outline, we obtain a constant succession of ups and downs in intensity, as in Chopin' *Nocturne in E flat:*

Nocturne, Op. 9, Nº 2   (Nº 41)   CHOPIN

Observe that in the above passage (with one slight exception) the points of melodic stress occur on the strong beats, so that pitch and rhythm coincide to emphasize the climaxes. When, however, the highest notes of the melody do not thus agree with the rhythmic accent, a new problem is presented which the player's good taste must solve. If, for instance, the highest note of the melody is especially important, it will take precedence of the measure accent at the climax point. In the following example from Mendelssohn's *Song without words*, No. 22, the first climax is best placed on the important C of the melody, while the second occurs on F, disregarding the less distinctive A, two notes before it:

Song without Words, Nº 22   (Nº 42)
Adagio   MENDELSSOHN

In general, it may be said that as the melody notes grow more rapid, less attention is paid to mere nuances of intensity and more to the rhythmic accent.

As with a melody, so an upward progression of chords or passage work normally suggests a crescendo, and a descending passage a diminuendo. For special effects, however, this principle may be contradicted, as in this excerpt from Chaminade's *Automne*, where a buoyant passage is tenderly echoed:

Automne, Op. 35, № 2   (№ 43)   CHAMINADE
Lento

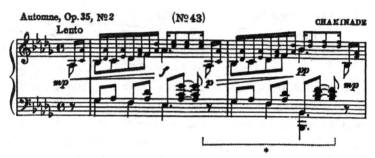

Conversely, a downward crescendo is sometimes utilized to produce a veritable avalanche of tone, as at the
outset of Grieg's *Concerto in A minor*, or the ending of
Liszt's *Rigoletto Paraphrase*.

Interrupted Climaxes

Occasionally, after a crescendo, our expectation of a
climax is suddenly thwarted by a soft chord. Beethoven
is fond of thus disappointing his auditors' expectations, as
in the *Andante* of his *Pastoral Sonata*, Op. 28:

Sonata, Op. 28   (№ 44)   BEETHOVEN
Andante

Similarly, Beethoven often precedes an entire soft section by a crescendo up to *forte*. This effect occurs several
times in the first movement of the *Pastoral Sonata* just
quoted.

Vitalizing Embellishments

It may be said that whenever a passage runs the danger of becoming flat and insipid to the hearer, it may be vitalized by the judicious use of crescendo and diminuendo. This is especially true of trills, which should never be presented in a lifeless manner. For example, the trills at the beginning of MacDowell's *Improvisation*, Op. 46, No. 4, should have a subtle crescendo, while the complex trill in the coda of Chopin's *Nocturne*, Op. 9, No. 2, calls for an ascending and descending wave.   Similarly, the frequent trills in the second movement of Haydn's *Sonata in F* (No. 20 in Peters Edition) should each have its slight growth or decrease in intensity.

VII.   Tempo

All the elements of rhythm and phrasing which we have discussed are finally controlled and regulated by the *tempo*, a term by which is meant (1) the rate of speed adopted for a given composition, and (2) the way in which this rate is managed by the player.   At the very foundation of consistent playing, indeed, is the employment of a movement that is neither so fast as to be unintelligible nor so slow as to become monotonous, and the maintenance of an even, steady swing that is modified or broken only when the exigencies of expression plainly demand it.

Tempo a Relative Factor

Let us agree at the outset that the rate of speed is not absolutely fixed for a given piece.   For just as two readers may interpret a poem equally well at different rates of utterance, so two pianists may each give an excellent rendition of the same piece, although their conceptions of its movement be different. To judge the merit of a performance, therefore, one has simply to ask whether or no it embodies the spirit and expression which was in the composer's mind.

For this reason, metronome marks, even if inserted by the composer, may be taken with considerable latitude. It might be well, indeed, if two sets of such marks were given for a composition, the one representing the maximum and the other the minimum limit of speed.

In their zeal to satisfy the metronome markings, students often attempt a rapidity that is far beyond their ability, and that consequently results in all sorts of errors in notes and technic. Remember, as Christiani aptly says, that "it is not so much a question of playing a great many notes with great velocity in a given degree of strength, as to play every note clearly, and in the spirit of the composition."[1] Better, therefore, disregard troublesome metronome marks, and confine your speed strictly to your ability!

Thus it is the general mood of a piece—lively, melancholy, peaceful—which should be the prime consideration. Most of the Italian terms associated with tempo, indeed, refer rather to the spirit of the performance than its rate. *Andante,* for instance, does not mean *slow,* but *walking along,* and *allegro* does not mean *fast,* but rather *gay* and *joyous.* Vivacity and brightness are never attained by mere speed; if this were so, the most eloquent preacher would be he who could talk the fastest. But precise and controlled rhythms, clear and pertinent accentuation — indicating a

[1]Christiani—*The Principles of Expression in Pianoforte Playing.*

strong heart-beat—will invest even a slow movement with abundant vitality.

Modification of Tempo

Fundamental steadiness, however, should not mean *stiffness* of tempo; for just as the apparently straight lines of the Parthenon at Athens have all been found to possess a slight curvature, so an apparently inflexible tempo, under the fingers of the artist, retains a subtle elasticity that invests it with human, rather than mechanical appeal.

Such elasticity has been suggested in our discussion of the agogic accent (page 28). While the latter slightly prolongs each first beat, however, the continual recurrence of this effect does not detract at all from the regular rhythmic swing. In compositions in which rhythm is the predominant factor, indeed, the pianist should be chary of disturbing the recurring heart-throb even to a slight degree. It is only when the lyric or dramatic moods of a singer are simulated that more latitude is allowed.

Hence in compositions in which the formal structure is emphasized, such as the polyphonic works of Bach and the sonatas of Haydn, Mozart and the early Beethoven, the strictness of the tempo should be little, if any, disturbed. We should except from this list, however, pieces by these composers in which the romantic school is plainly forecast, such as Bach's *Chromatic Fantasy*.

Tempo modification in endings is generally regarded as permissible in both classic and modern music. In the time of Bach, for instance, dignity was added to the close of a composition by a rallentando in the final cadence. In bravura music, however, a final crescendo is intensified by a corresponding acceleration — *vide* Beethoven's *Sonata*, Op. 13, or Moszkowski's *Air de Ballet*, Op. 36, No. 5. Conversely, a gradual retard emphasizes the restful effect of a final diminuendo, as in the close of Grieg's *Berceuse*.

Without question, the lyric passages which occur especially in Beethoven's slow movements should be played with a certain emotional freedom; but "in playing great works, works continuous and large in their construction, such as are Beethoven's, we must often restrain the impulse to color each detail too strongly, lest we lose sight of the larger shapes of the piece, its general feeling and the majestic progression of its great proportions."[1]   So in the works of all the great masters, from pre-Bach days to the present, the emotional values must, in the final analysis, control mere tempo limitations — despite the contention of so-called "classicists," who would play the works of dead composers as though the inspiration of their compositions had been buried with them! Even Mendelssohn, stickler for rigid tempo that he was, must have relaxed his own principles when inspired by the moods of some of his *Songs without Words*. In a wild flight of fancy, indeed, he treats the sedate fugue with a continual acceleration in his Op. 35, No. 1!

Tempo Rubato

While Schumann's frequent marks of tempo-changes prove his own freedom from the strait-jacket of strict time,

[1]Matthay—*Musical Interpretation.*

it was Chopin who boldly proclaimed the virtues of a judicious *tempo rubato*.

Meaning literally *changing time*, the tempo rubato of Chopin has commonly been interpreted to signify a slight fluctuation, in which an accelerando is compensated for by a corresponding ritardando, or *vice versa*. Thus if the same phrase were begun simultaneously by two persons, one of whom played rubato and the other in strict time, they would play the final note in unison.

Hence, by the use of rubato, a pianist may handle an emotional melody with a singer's plasticity, in which, gracefully soaring up to each little climax, the voice poises upon it for an instant, and then flutters down like an autumn leaf. For example, consider the first phrase of the *Nocturne in B major*:

Occasionally the rubato is used for a highly dramatic effect, as in an ensuing phrase of the same nocturne:

Especially susceptible to rubato are those vocal-like cadenzas which are frequent in Chopin's lyrics, and to which he purposely refrained from assigning exact time-values. Here is an example from the *Nocturne in F♯*:

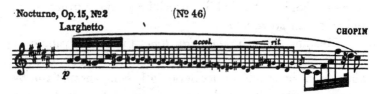

Nocturne, Op. 15, Nº 2   (Nº 46)

Larghetto   CHOPIN

In applying the rubato, one should pay due regard to Chopin's injunction that while the melody is thus bent, the accompaniment should retain its steadfast swing. True, a too literal interpretation of this rule might result in an awkward confusion between the two hands. Doubtless, however, Chopin sought by this means to restrain the exuberant student from exaggerating an effect which should be employed with extreme subtlety. Illustrating right and wrong rubato to a pupil, Chopin is said to have first blown upon a candle flame so gently that it only flickered, saying, "See, this is my rubato;" after which he blew out the flame, saying, "and that is your rubato."

In Chopin's waltzes and polonaises especially, the rubato should not be allowed to interfere with the rhythmic stability. But with the mazurkas, saturated by the fitful moods of the Slav, greater liberty is natural. Sometimes, for instance, the mood now dwells on a pompous crisis, and now dashes recklessly on; as in the *Mazurka in B♭*, where a lingering crescendo incites a lively reaction:

Mazurka, Op. 7, Nº 1   (Nº 47)

Vivace   CHOPIN

Such a free treatment of tempo may in a measure justify the contention of some musicians that the compensation of an accellerando by a ritardando is not necessary, and that, if pushed too far, such a rule nullifies the very freedom which rubato is intended to afford. No doubt this "robbing Peter to pay Paul" may be carried to a pedantic limit; but its underlying principle is a just one, since by such compensation that rhythmic symmetry is preserved which is a fundamental feature of musical structure, without which a composition is merely a fitful succession of unrelated details. It is this very incoherent use of rubato, indeed, that has made it such a dangerous weapon in the hands of unskilled, "temperamental" amateurs, and which should be shunned as an instance not of justified liberty, but of unrestrained license.

VIII. COLOR

A watchword of modern composition and interpretation is *color*. Borrowed from the art of painting, its musical significance is somewhat vague; but in the common acceptance of the term it refers primarily to distinctive *qualities of tone*—such as those of the clarinet, horn and violin—and only secondarily to different tints of the same general color, such as are represented by varying degrees of *forte* and *piano*.

Hence in the primary sense, the chief medium for coloristic effects is the orchestra, in which many distinct qualities of tone are available for the composer's palette, and which he may mingle or distinguish according to the promptings of his genius.

On the piano, however, owing to the limited range of quality that is available, we must often fall back upon the secondary meaning that has been mentioned, and create the *illusion* of different hues by dynamic contrasts and shadings. How these factors may be utilized by the player has already been described. It remains, therefore, to investigate just what varieties of quality are to be found in the instrument, and to what extent these may be employed as factors in expression.

Tone in the piano is produced by the stroke of the hammer against its string — or, rather, its three strings. Also, whatever the propelling force, the hammer always strikes its strings at exactly the same place.

For this hammer stroke, the direct propelling power lies in the key-lever, which may be depressed at its outer end by the player's finger only about three-eighths of an inch. During this key-depression the hammer is rising at a much more rapid rate, until it arrives at a point near the string, when the motive power of the key stops, since the key has reached its key-bed; and the hammer is thus left to fly the rest of the way to the string, actuated by the *momentum already imparted to it*. It is important that this last statement be well understood, since it means that the really effective part of the hammer-stroke is actually *without the control of the player*.

Observe, then, that a given degree of force behind the hammer-stroke *will always produce the same tone*, however the key is depressed, whether its descent begins slowly and accelerates, whether it begins quickly and slows up, or whether it descends at a fixed rate. Hence the popular conception that different kinds of tone, familiarly described as *rich, velvety, dry, dull*, etc., are produced by causing the hammer to press the string, to strike it indirectly and the like, are quite contrary to fact; so that these tonal varieties must be accounted for in other ways.

But while a hammer-stroke of a given degree of force always evokes the same quality of tone from its strings, it is nevertheless true that the quality is *not* the same when different degrees of force are applied. Strike a key down violently, and a sharp tone results, caused by bright upper partials (or secondary vibrations of the string) which are thus called into action. Press the key down gently, and the tone will not only soften, but will also differ in quality, since the more remote upper partials are no longer aroused. Between these two extremes are a host of slightly differing qualities, according as certain upper partials appear or disappear.

Two pianists will naturally employ a different range of force, hence their playing will correspondingly differ in its apparent quality. Miss A, for instance, whose touch is habitually quick and nervous, evokes more of the sharper upper partials than Miss B, who plays with a more reticant touch. Miss A, therefore, makes the piano sound brilliant, and Miss B mellow.

Also, when two or more tones are sounded simultaneously, the result is a mixture of their individual qualities; and this mixture will vary according as the two tones are of the same or different strength. Quality combinations may in this way change indefinitely, and will depend upon the executant's skill and taste in selecting just the right tonal values (see page 21).

Effect of Legato and Staccato

We may here mention a factor which plays a considerable part in creating the illusion of different qualities—namely, the connection or disconnection between successive tones. If the notes of a melody are played staccato, each stands out in sharp relief from its fellows. Closer connection, however, may be either of three kinds: the *non-legato*, in which the tones are just separated, the *legato proper*, in which they exactly meet, and the *legatissimo*, in which they overlap. Representing the tones by circles, these three kinds may be thus graphically indicated: (1) ◯◯◯ (2) ◯◯◯ (3) ◖◗◖◗

A certain apparent dryness of tone, resulting from the first kind, is softened down by the second kind; while in the third kind one tone mingles for an instant with the next, like a dissolving view. Hence in the formal and obvious types of music—like that of Bach, Haydn and Mozart—the first two kinds are almost exclusively employed, while with the romantic composers, notably Chopin, the blending of outlines suggests the legatissimo.

Supplemental Noises

There are certain factors, too, which modify the tone-quality of the string itself. One of these is the *noise of the key-mechanism*, which is determined by the grade and condition of the piano. In instruments of the higher grade this noise is reduced to a minimum by careful adjustment of the action. Even the best of pianos, however, without proper care is apt to develop squeaks and clicks of the action which interfere seriously with the tonal beauty.

More under the control of the player are the noises caused by the method of attacking the keys. An argument in favor of reducing to a minimum the stroke of the fingers lies in the fact that this stroke involves an unpleasant noise which mingles with the legitimate tone.

Close the piano lid, and try playing upon it with a forcible finger action. The result is a succession of thuds, loud enough to be heard in the adjoining room. When such a finger stroke is extensively employed, therefore, these thuds have a very decided effect for the worse on the tone-quality.

Pedals

For variety in quality, however, the modern pianist relies chiefly on the pedals. By depressing the right or *damper* pedal, he lifts all of the dampers from the strings, so that not only do the tones produced continue to vibrate, but also the quality of these tones is altered by the sympathetic vibration of other strings.

Without sounding them, press down Middle *c, e* and *g*:

with the right hand. Sustain these keys, and at the same time play bass C:

with a sharp staccato. You will then hear the whole chord *c, e, g*, which sounds in sympathy with the upper partials of the bass C.

Again, when the left or *soft* pedal on the grand piano is depressed, the action is moved to the right, so that each hammer strikes two, instead of three strings. Not only is the tone thus softened, but its quality is altered both by the new relation of the felts on the hammers to the strings, and also by the sympathetic vibration of the third (free) string.

We need not here discuss the third pedal, which is

present on most modern pianos, since its office in sustaining individual tones has no new effect on tone-quality.

Summary

Actual changes in tone-quality, therefore, occur:

1.   When a key is depressed with different degrees of force.

2.   When two or more tones are mingled in different proportions.

3.   When the noise of the finger-stroke on the key mingles with the tone.

4.   When the pedals are used, either separately or in combination.

If we add to this list the effects produced by dynamics and by gradations of staccato and legato, it is plain that the pianist possesses a considerable store of coloristic devices which, if properly handled, may largely atone for the limitations of the piano in regard to tone-quality, and which may at least create the illusion of a wide range of hues and shadings.[1]

IX. Style

Ultimately, the manner in which the player correlates the factors of touch and expression constitutes his *individual style*. If he lays too great emphasis on technic, his style will be cold and unfeeling. On the other hand, emotional expression without adequate technic results in an overdrawn

[1]For a convincing treatment of the subject discussed in this section, the reader is referred to the admirable book by Otto Ortmann, entitled *The Physical Basis of Touch and Tone.*

and slovenly style. In contrast to either of these extremes is the well-balanced playing of an artist whose competent technic is accompanied by an equally sane use of all the factors of expression.

For our purpose, however, we may consider style as compounded of three factors, each one of which is necessary for a well-rounded interpretation. These factors are: (1) accuracy in rendering the notes, (2) fidelity to the composer's intentions, and (3) the player's own personality.

Accuracy

Perhaps the nervous hurry of our American life is responsible for the insistent search for short cuts to perfection. "I have only six months to spend," says an ambitious student, "and must learn to play difficult music in that time." Hence a mad scramble to grasp as many pieces as possible, with a consequent slurring of details in order to obtain a specious general effect. One such student informed me that she had been practicing an entire new sonata of Beethoven for each weekly lesson!

Let me quote the advice to teachers given by Mr. Arthur Foote: "Have your pupil realize that while playing that is accurate may possess no other value, it is the material out of which musical playing can be made; that which is inaccurate cannot possibly be musical."[1]

To strike the correct notes is only one of several factors necessary to accuracy of playing. Each note and also each *rest* (page 45) must be given its required time-value; a

[1]Article, *Can Expressive Playing be Taught?*, in the *Étude* for March, 1926.

definite fingering must be adopted; and the proper touch must be decided on. Lastly, these mere mechanical details must be made to meet the demands of phrasing, tempo, dynamics and the like, before the piece is ready for the finishing touches.

Intentions of the Composer

In evolving a consistent interpretation of a piece, the student should make careful use of every indication given by the composer as to his own wishes. Unfortunately, in pre-Beethoven music expression marks are few and of a merely general character, such as *piano* and *forte*. But from Beethoven on, the indications rapidly increase, until, with the exception of the slurs (page 31), they become a constant and safe guide. One must, however, guard against confusing the genuine indications given by the composer with the misleading markings of many of the so-called "critical editions." In many German editions of the late nineteenth century, for instance, the theory is insisted upon that a finger should always be changed when a note is repeated, notwithstanding the frequent absurdity of such a proceeding. Even the most scholarly editions, therefore, should be accepted with a grain of salt, and tested by the light of the student's own musical experience.

Another highly important guide to interpretation is found in the study of how piano music has gradually evolved; what forms and styles it has assumed at different epochs; and what were the ideals and resources of its composers. To play Debussy in the style of Bach or Mozart, for instance, is as great an anachronism as to wear at the present time the garments in vogue during the eighteenth century.[1]

Personality

But even the most explicit notation falls far short of completeness. It is just as impossible, indeed, to indicate on the written music every slight nuance of expression as it would be to show every inflection of the voice in the report of an orator's speech. Hence the final factor of interpretation must be found in the personality of the player—in his individual reaction to the spirit of the piece, after he has mastered its intricate details, and has viewed them, as far as possible, from the composer's stand-point. Each pianist, in other words, must ultimately round out his interpretation in the light of his own intelligence and emotions. Providing, then, that the result is consistent, it is quite justified, even if it vary considerably from that of other pianists. "If only one correct rendition of a composition were possible," said Wagner, "the executive artist would be a mere monkey."

Not only, indeed, do different players present varied interpretations of the same piece, but the same player, under diverse circumstances, may quite perceptibly alter his own version.[2] What pianist, when inspired by an enthusiastic audience, has not introduced unexpected effects of rhythmic variation, of stress upon certain notes, of delicate contrasts,

[1] The reader is here referred to the volume, *Piano Music: Its Composers and Characteristics*, by the author of this book.

[2] One of his pupils declared that "Chopin's interpretation of his own music was never twice alike, yet always perfect." No doubt a similar statement could be made regarding the playing of Liszt, Rubinstein, and others of the great virtuosi.

which were revealed to him in a sudden flash of genius! In so doing, he demonstrates the fact that the very creation of the piece has passed from the hands of the composer to his own: that he has so absorbed every item of its execution as to relegate it to his sub-conscious mind, while he speaks directly to his audience in terms of his own personality.

This is the point, then, to which all our study of touch and expression must lead us if it is to be of any real value. For it is only when the meticulous details are blended and coördinated into one consistent whole that they truly voice the artistic impulse of the performer, and that they become the fitting vehicle of "art for art's sake."

INDEX

69